WELCOME TO DALLAS, MR. KENNEDY

Welcome to Dallas, Mr. Kennedy is a biting satire that uses the first Kennedy assassination to tilt at the capitalist structure of U.S. society and the paranoid Right-Wing atmospheres it creates. In the form of a revue, it recreates the events immediately leading up to the fatal motorcade in Dallas in November, 1963, and intersperses them with a savage exposé of U.S. attitudes to Communism, Fidel Castro, the global power struggle, civil rights and the military/industrial complex, whose activities Gen. Eisenhower warned against in his last speech as President in 1959. John F. Kennedy's public image as a 'liberal idealist' is exposed as largely an illusion, manufactured by U.S. capitalists to disguise the true nature of their society from its victims. This controversial and hard-hitting play, written in 1967, also succeeds in illuminating the root causes of the present political mood of extreme conservatism in the U.S.A. and the violence that seems endemic to U.S. life, which since 1963 has accounted for Malcolm X, Martin Luther King and Robert F. Kennedy among others. Its savage attack on the findings of the Warren Commission, which in the author's opinion represented a closing of ranks by the U.S. Establishment to cover up the truth, reinforces Himmelstrup's view of a corrupt society based on false values that he communicates with a violent irony.

Kaj Himmelstrup has written several plays, many of which have been performed in the theatre and on television in Denmark. A story he wrote for children, The Children of Tonacatecutli, has been translated into English and published in Great Britain by The Bodley Head. He makes his living as a teacher in a small experimental school in Denmark.

CALDER AND BOYARS · LONDON

First published in Great Britain 1971
by Calder and Boyars Ltd
18 Brewer Street London W1R 4AS

ISBN 0 7145 0776 8 Cloth Edition
ISBN 0 7145 0777 6 Paper Edition

Printed by photo-lithography
and made in Great Britain at
The Pitman Press, Bath.

WELCOME TO DALLAS, MR. KENNEDY

WELCOME TO DALLAS, MR. KENNEDY was first performed in November, 1967, at the Fiol Teatret, Copenhagen, with the following cast:

Beatrice Bonnesen, Birgit Brüel, Katja Miehe-Renard, Olaf Nielsen, Finn Poulsen, Ole Kjaer.

The play was directed by Finn Henning Poulsen.

Editor's Note:

The slides, cartoon film and Vietnam film mentioned in the script are available for hire by theatre companies performing this play from C and B (Theatre) Ltd., 18 Brewer Street, London, W1R 4AS. The fee, which is very moderate, can be included in the fee for the rights to perform the play.

(Before the curtain rises, 'Elm Street Blues' is played on a tape-recorder. The music fades...)

A VOICE. Ladies and gentlemen, you are now listening to Elm Street Blues, recorded in Dallas in the state of Texas in that fateful year 1929.

(The music fades in again. When the tune is finished, a spotlight goes up on the curtain. Silence. The curtain rises)

MAN. They don't need to hold so tight, I'm not running off anywhere. How could I? - They talk to me all the time, I'm supposed to answer. Question after question, when one of them has finished the next one starts. They want to know everything. Suddenly they begin asking me about the same things all over again, it never stops. - They say a police officer has been shot. He was driving along in a patrol car, quite slowly, then drew in to the right, stopped by the pavement and wound down the window. He said something to a man, then got out of the car and was shot. They say it was me. They've got eye-witnesses, they say. Four times I've been down to the basement. They stand me in a long line with police in plain clothes and the witnesses stand along the opposite wall behind a big nylon screen so they can't be seen. A little while later the detectives come back. That's good enough, they say, you've been recognized. Then they start up again. I don't know how long it's been going on. They've taken my watch - it's so I don't break the glass and cut my wrists, according to them. We're looking after you. Nothing must happen to you. You're damn well not going to croak before your time. It was you who murdered Kennedy, we've a lot on you, loads of evidence, a revolver, a rifle, finger prints, witnesses' testimony, photographs, we've had people in the chair for less. And then, you've been to Russia, you swine, but wait a minute - you've already hit the headlines, Lee - you're exposed. I'm on the front page, millions of front pages. People'll know who killed Kennedy - (signal from car horn) - It wasn't me - (shot)

(The MAN stiffens into the position shown on the newspaper picture and holds this position throughout the following)

2ND WOMAN. You filthy rat, you skunk, you killed the president, Jackie's husband. You got what was coming to you. New headlines, new front page...

(Organ plays the introduction to the song, boogie-woogie tempo)

Fantastically on target, you're getting Oswald's
(murder hot
While they're taking photos of him, at that moment
(he gets shot

You'll admit that for a press scoop it surely beats
(the lot
And as for police service, it's the best we've ever
(got
Though it's pretty clear the police had been informed
(about the plot
For a newspaper, I tell you, it's a dream. Wow.
On the front page you have Ruby, pistol smoking at
(his side
And of other bits of news too, the variety is wide
It only took one bullet to pierce our murderer's
(hide
He owns a nightclub, Ruby, where the strippers'
(trade is plied
We promise you we'll find out if he's anything to
(hide
For a newspaper, I tell you, it's a dream. Wow.

(1ST WOMAN takes a sheet out of the chest)

2ND WOMAN. What's that?

1ST WOMAN. The veil of oblivion. (she puts it over the MAN) News fades fast. Come on.

2ND WOMAN. New headlines - on the 22nd, Kennedy murdered, the 23rd, Oswald charged, the 24th, Ruby shoots Oswald - the same day as the funeral, that's a damned cheek. The 25th. What shall we use on the 25th?

1ST WOMAN. Ruby?

2ND WOMAN. O.K., we'll use Ruby. The 26th?

1ST WOMAN. More about Ruby?

2ND WOMAN. No. New headlines.

1ST WOMAN. Why not?

2ND WOMAN. It'll be the third day running. They don't feel like hearing any more about Ruby. He's not saying anything, just jawing on. There's nothing meaty on Ruby. What else happened on the 26th?

1ST WOMAN. Kennedy's race bill defeated in Congress?

2ND WOMAN. Idiot, that's not front page material.

1ST WOMAN. Rumours, conjectures?

2ND WOMAN. Excellent. The 27th?

1ST WOMAN. More rumours? - How about a conspiracy?

2ND WOMAN. Not bad, but then I don't think we can stretch that any further. The 28th?

1ST WOMAN. What's the new president saying?

2ND WOMAN. Nothing. The 29th?

1ST WOMAN. Johnson appoints a big commission, with Warren, the President of the Supreme Court, in the chair. The murder's going to be fully investigated.

2ND WOMAN. That's just two small columns on page three. I'm talking about the front page, you know. Come on, it's the damned front page that sells. They're sitting waiting. You needn't look at me. Hell, there's nothing wrong with me, it's them. New headlines, new front page. I know

quite well what you're saying about me. I'm
sensation mad, superficial, fickle, I rush about
from one thing to another, letting events die in
my wake from day to day - you just sneer...

(Organ music for song)

A paper is a mirror, so you needn't strain your
(eye
It's fun you want, amusement, just a glance will
(get you by

1ST WOMAN. (ironically)
You have to skim the surface, it's such a shame,
(you sigh
You'd much, much rather view in depth, ask what
(and how and why

2ND WOMAN.
Of course, but good intentions just don't keep the
(sales high
For a newspaper, I tell you, that is death. Wow.
That's why we carefully give you everything you're
(waiting for
The daily, penny-dreadful stuff, sensations, chaos,
(war
Train accidents, bombs over Laos, the fire
(engine's roar
And if you get tired of that we'll give you what you
(all adore
Your royal marriages and births, joy no one can
(ignore
For a newspaper, that's what it's all about. Wow.
Then a year after the murder, to the highly
(impatient nation
The commission under Warren issued its lengthy
(dissertation
But as ill luck would have it, the thing's far from

(a sensation
He was acting on his own, the man they killed at
(the police station
As far as he's concerned there will be no more
(agitation
For a newspaper he's ancient history now.

(During the last verse, 1ST WOMAN has taken a big picture of the Warren Commission out of the chest and hung it on the wall. Now she takes out a telegram)

1ST WOMAN. New headlines, new front page, military coup in Greece - the Junta has seized power because the populace wasn't ripe for democracy. (to the audience) You'll have to do something about that, won't you? I'm sure you have, haven't you, sir? Your conscience wouldn't give you any peace otherwise, would it? We must condemn their action, protest about it - we'll have to shake up our politicians, get them to really intervene. After all, we're bound to succeed, we've got the press behind us.

2ND WOMAN. New headlines, new front page, Israel starts a blitzkrieg against Egypt. Wow, seven columns, finest picture coverage, empty boots in the desert, camp morale, yum-yum - six hectic days at the news desk, bravely we fight our way through the cables, we made it - Nasser bites the dust... (long sigh of relief)

1ST WOMAN. And democracy in Greece?

2ND WOMAN. What? Is that news?

MAN. And me?

2ND WOMAN. You?

MAN. Yes, what about me?

2ND WOMAN. Oh you - you're dead and buried, my friend, forgotten.

MAN. I want to be exhumed.

2ND WOMAN. Never. You would have finished in the chair anyway. A foot-note in world history.

MAN. That's not true.

2ND WOMAN. The Warren Commission condemned you.

MAN. Condemned? Was it a trial, then?

2ND WOMAN. You didn't have the ghost of a chance. Read the Warren Report - 26 volumes altogether, with cross examinations.

MAN. Other books have come out.

2ND WOMAN. All right, all right.

MAN. Which you ought to have written.

2ND WOMAN. Me?

MAN. Aren't you the custodian of the truth? the bloodhound of justice? the conscience of the nation?

2ND WOMAN. Why shouldn't we believe the Warren Report?

MAN. Have you read it?

(A pause)

1ST WOMAN. Don't you think you ought to give him a chance?

2ND WOMAN. O.K., then, let's start all over again. Dallas, on the 22nd November, 1963.

(MAN stands up. The sheet unfolds into a Kukluxklan robe. On the front of it a slide is shown: an anti-Kennedy advertisement from a Dallas newspaper)

MAN. Welcome to Dallas, Mr. Kennedy. We are saying hello with a series of small questions in the morning paper, a whole-page advertisement with a black border. Why - why - why -

1ST WOMAN. Why have you ordered your brother Bobby to go soft on the communists?

MAN. Why are your critics persecuted?

1ST WOMAN. The head of the American Communist Party praises all your policies, Mr. Kennedy. Why?

MAN. Why will he support your re-election in 1964?

1ST WOMAN. Why are seven million Cubans living in communist slavery, Mr. Kennedy?

MAN. It's your fault. Why are you betraying the proud tradition of freedom in the United States in favour of the 'Spirit of Moscow'?

WANTED

FOR

TREASON

THIS MAN is wanted for treasonous activities against the United States:

1. Betraying the Constitution (which he swore to uphold):
   He is turning the sovereignty of the U. S. over to the communist controlled United Nations.
   He is betraying our friends (Cuba, Katanga, Portugal) and befriending our enemies (Russia, Yugoslavia, Poland).
2. He has been WRONG on innumerable issues affecting the security of the U.S. (United Nations-Berlin wall-Missle removal-Cuba-Wheat deals-Test Ban Treaty, etc.)
3. He has been lax in enforcing Communist Registration laws.
4. He has given support and encouragement to the Communist inspired racial riots.
5. He has illegally invaded a sovereign State with federal troops.
6. He has consistently appointed Anti-Christians to Federal office: Upholds the Supreme Court in its Anti-Christian rulings.
   Aliens and known Communists abound in Federal offices.
7. He has been caught in fantastic LIES to the American people (including personal ones like his previous marraige and divorce).

This handbill was distributed in Dallas the day before the murder. 5,000 copies were printed, according to the Warren Commission, by the 38-year-old printer Robert A. Surrey who was closely connected with the ultra-conservative General Edwin A. Walker and thus with the notorious John Birch Society.

1ST WOMAN. Why are you letting the world turn towards the left?

MAN. Why are you selling wheat to our communist enemies?

1ST WOMAN. They're the same enemies who are killing our boys in Vietnam.

(MAN throws off the sheet and stands with the Dallas Morning News in his hand)

MAN. Jackie?

1ST WOMAN. Mmm.

MAN. We've come to the Wild West, Jackie, right out where the buffalo roam. (he gives her the paper, shaking his head) What do you think these people really look like, inside?

1ST WOMAN. (reading, lowers the paper) Why are you letting the world turn towards the left?

MAN. What are you thinking about?

1ST WOMAN. Don't you think we'd better ask to have the bullet-proof roof on the car?

MAN. But darling, what about your new hat?

1ST WOMAN. I'm being serious, Jack.

MAN. All right, so then what? If someone wants to shoot their president, they can go into a shop anywhere and buy a rifle, then all they have to do is sit at a window when I'm driving past and not a living soul'll be able to stop it happening. -

It's strange but it honestly is true. We were talking about it an hour before it happened. - A bullet-proof roof's no guarantee of safety, either. Besides it'd be bad psychology.

1ST WOMAN. Why did we have to come to Texas?

MAN. The party is cracking up, and we can't afford that down here.

1ST WOMAN. Why do _you_ have to stick it together again?

MAN. That was a good speech you made to the Latin Americans yesterday - in Spanish too. That kind of thing means something.

1ST WOMAN. Why couldn't Johnson do it himself?

MAN. They've hung paintings up in the hotel, to please us. Wasn't that nice of them? I'd say they've emptied their museum.

1ST WOMAN. Johnson's a Texan.

MAN. Good God, Jackie, I have to give him a boost, too. It's as routine as that... Give me a smile... You'll have to smile for Dallas, anyway.

1ST WOMAN. They spat on Stevenson when he was here.

2ND WOMAN. (with a pile of handbills) This man is wanted, J. F. K., guilty of treason. He is offending our allies in Katanga and Portugal and currying favour with our enemies in Russia and Poland. He is filling the government offices with anti-christians and supporting the communist racial riots. He tells fantastic lies to the American people and keeps things secret. (whispering) Have you ever heard about his first marriage and divorce?

(She scatters the handbills freely among the audience)

MAN. Darling, they've given you a pair of Texan boots and a ten gallon hat. They really like you, you know? - We'll be landing soon.

2ND WOMAN. Please fasten your seat belts.

MAN. What's the airport called?

2ND WOMAN. (amorously) Love Field... can you beat it?

(MAN and 1ST WOMAN get up from their stools to meet the 3RD WOMAN who presents flowers to 1ST WOMAN. MAN radiates vitality, walks along footlights)

MAN. The Kennedy style - How is your old mother? - Vote for Kennedy next time, will you? - This is a lovely town you have here - You do vote for me, thank you - Don't forget the old people - You're a teacher? Better schools for our children, that's my programme, higher pay for teachers - This is my wife Jackie - I beg your pardon? No, she isn't pregnant. - I'll do my best. - Vote for me, thank you.

(MAN and 1ST WOMAN sit beside each other on the chest. 2ND and 3RD WOMAN are out at the side on stools)

1ST WOMAN. (cheerful) Then we sit in the car, a big Lincoln with red leather seats. In front of us sit Governor Connally and his wife. She's called Nellie - she has nice eyes - and in front of them sits the chauffeur. He's called Greer, I think, and beside him sits Kellerman, the only secret service man. We haven't any security men on the running board and none behind us either, just Johnson. (they wave) Jack's taught me how to change hands so that I don't grow tired. That's why I've put the roses down between us. It's funny - you learn to look on it as a kind of job. It can be rationally organized, he takes that side and I look after this one.

MAN. (smiling and waving) It's a hellishly ugly place, Dallas. An upstart town. Three-quarters of a million inhabitants, half of them trash, at least. No culture. - Mockingbird Lane, Lemmon Avenue, then we turn in to Turtle Creek and Cedar Springs - that sounds romantic, probably all the romance there is in Dallas. (he pats 1ST WOMAN's hand) We're getting near the centre, Main Street, banks and oil firms.

3RD WOMAN. Mercantile Building. Hunt the oil millionaire between two beautiful secretaries.

MAN. Hunt - a good name in that business.

1ST WOMAN. Nellie turns round and smiles.

2ND WOMAN. (turning) They can't hear him, she says to herself, but he sits and says thank you just the same. Thank you - it must be something to do with his upbringing.

3RD WOMAN. Now they're driving out on to Dealey

Plaza. It's not very beautiful here but you have to put the warehouses somewhere. The big clock up on the roof says 12.30 - in five minutes they'll be in Trade Mart and the speech is ready.

(MAN feels in his inside pocket)

2ND WOMAN. This may be all the Democrats there are in Dallas gathered here, but there are an amazing number of them.

1ST WOMAN. Now Nellie turns round again and smiles at Jack.

2ND WOMAN. (turns round, smiles) You certainly can't say that the people of Dallas haven't given you a nice welcome, Mr. President.

MAN. No, you certainly can't.

(Hiss on the organ. MAN clutches at his neck. The following must be said very quickly but coldly, clinically)

3RD WOMAN. Suddenly the President grabs at his neck.

2ND WOMAN. Everybody hears a loud bang, but most people think it's fireworks...

1ST WOMAN. ... or the back fire of a motor cycle. There's always a lot of noise when you've driving in a motorcade.

3RD WOMAN. Connally turns round to the right to look out the back.

1ST WOMAN. It's terribly hot and they have been

waving for forty minutes.

3RD WOMAN. He's an old soldier and recognizes a rifle shot.

1ST WOMAN. And Nellie has heard the bang too, and looks back over her shoulder. The President still has his hand up to his neck - Jackie is looking out over the square. If only she was allowed to put her sunglasses on.

3RD WOMAN. Then Connally turns round to the left.

1ST WOMAN. Oh no no no, he shouts, they are going to kill us all.

3RD WOMAN. His shirt is covered in blood, and he falls screaming into Nellie's lap.

1ST WOMAN. Jackie has turned round and is looking at her husband. He has such an odd look on his face, as if there was something he doesn't understand. And at the same time that nauseating sound, like a pineapple that has been thrown against a wall, and he lifts up his hand as if to smooth back his hair and she sees a piece of his skull and for a long time afterwards she remembers that it's the colour of flesh. There isn't any blood, it's nice and clean, but there's a piece about five inches long missing that's broken off - and then he falls slowly into her lap.

2ND WOMAN. And Nellie hears her scream: They have shot my husband, they have shot my husband - notice she says 'they' - They have shot him, I have brains on my fingers.

3RD WOMAN. Kellerman on the front seat hasn't

heard anything, but finally he wakes up. He calls over the radio, Let's get out of here, take us to a hospital.

1ST WOMAN. And while Greer's speeding up and the motorcade goes haywire, police chief Curry asks the base station to notify Parkland Hospital on Stemmons Freeway.

2ND WOMAN. But when the man on duty presses the button, it sticks and the hospital isn't alerted until Kennedy's car arrives, surrounded by motor cycles with blaring sirens.

(Siren noises on the organ)

3RD WOMAN. At 12.38 an entry is made in tidy handwriting: John F. Kennedy, white, male, principal injury bullet wound.

2ND WOMAN. At one o'clock the doctors give up hope... poor Mrs. Kennedy.

3RD WOMAN. It was the ninety-ninth murder in Dallas that year.

(The siren noises become Elm Street Blues)

2nd WOMAN. Ladies and gentlemen, Elm Street Blues:

Dallas, not a cheer; Elm Street, nothing near
A verse for the young president who comes driving
(here
Dallas, hate and shock; Elm Street coldly mocks
The young president in the noon heat at twelve by
(the clock
Dallas raised its hand, Elm Street, blood-filled

(land
What was it the young president didn't understand?

MAN. Well - we might as well stop here, since it's just this very question we want to have settled. Why was he so amazed by that shot? But then, on the other hand, I suppose we ought to get Kennedy out of Dallas, so we'll have two more scenes. Johnson has arrived at the hospital surrounded by secret service people - before Kennedy, by the way. He's safe in the medical ward and isn't allowed to leave it. Only Mrs. Johnson is given permission to leave the room. 'See if you can find Jackie and Nellie, comfort them a bit'.

(3RD WOMAN starts to walk away, suddenly thinks of something)

3RD WOMAN. Ah, my book.

MAN. Your book?

3RD WOMAN. (finds book in chest) 'The never-to-be-forgotten moment'... How do I find the way to...

2ND WOMAN. You follow the red line along the corridor, ma'am.

(3RD WOMAN looks down in front of her, walks on the spot, stops in front of 1ST WOMAN who is sitting on a stool staring through her)

3RD WOMAN. Is that the operating theatre? (no answer) Why don't you take off your gloves? There's blood on them.

1ST WOMAN. I'm so glad I was with him. Supposing I hadn't been there.

3RD WOMAN. Mrs. Kennedy, we didn't want this to happen, you believe that, don't you? - Not in that way, anyhow.

1ST WOMAN. If I'd turned round a little earlier - or if I'd just - I could have managed it.

(3RD WOMAN turns and catches sight of 2ND WOMAN. She embraces her warmly)

3RD WOMAN. Oh Nellie, what a terrible business about John, but it'll be all right in the end, he'll recover.

2ND WOMAN. He will, Bird.

3RD WOMAN. I'm telling you, her dress was spattered all over with blood and she was the one who always made such a point of being spotless, and her gloves weren't just covered, they were caked with it... I've never got used to wearing gloves, it's not my style at all, but she's like that, I...

2ND WOMAN. They say he'll pull through.

3RD WOMAN. Of course he will, darling, of course. I bet you he'll be going strong at ninety. See you, Nellie. Lyndon is waiting. It'll be the first time I've ever been in the presidential plane, Air Force One.

1ST WOMAN. (to MAN) Kellerman, you've known Jack for a long time - did I do right? That was my wedding ring. He bought it in Newport just before our wedding. There wasn't even time to have the date put on. I got that done afterwards. Was it wrong to leave it with him in the coffin?

MAN. I think it was right, Mrs. Kennedy. Wouldn't you rather drive out to the plane now?

1ST WOMAN. I'm not going home before I have Jack with me.

(3RD WOMAN takes a plastic bag from the chest and waddles over to 1ST WOMAN. MAN tries to stop her, but she won't be put off)

3RD WOMAN. Peter Cain, dominican abbot at the Catholic University of Dallas. The president was a Catholic, so I can surely lend a hand here. (to 1ST WOMAN) When did he die?

1ST WOMAN. In the car, I suppose.

3RD WOMAN. Sad, sad, but we all have to go the same way. Now take a look at what I have here - (opens the bag) - a splinter of the True Cross. Perhaps you would care to pay reverence to it? Si capex, ego te absolvo e peccatis tuis, in nomine patris et filii et spiritus sancti. (she makes as if to kneel but decides not to) He's bled a bit, hasn't he? It's appalling, Jackie, I know how you must be feeling - I think I will write to you.

(MAN forces her away)

MAN. We are ready to go now.

2ND WOMAN. No you're not.

MAN. Come on.

2ND WOMAN. You're not going anywhere with that coffin.

MAN. Who are you?

2ND WOMAN. Earl Rose, District Medical Officer of Dallas.

MAN. Roy Kellerman, secret service.

2ND WOMAN. There has been a murder here. You are not allowed to leave before an autopsy has taken place.

MAN. My dear man, this is the late president, and we are taking him home with us to Washington.

2ND WOMAN. You can't do that. According to Texas law, an autopsy must be carried out after a murder. We'll have to take the lid off.

MAN. The president is coming with us now.

2ND WOMAN. You people from Washington can't have your own laws. The body stays here.

MAN. (with a gesture towards 1ST WOMAN) Couldn't you show some consideration?

2ND WOMAN. Mrs. Kennedy can do whatever she likes. She isn't being accused of anything.

MAN. We are leaving now.

2ND WOMAN. For Christ's sake, a murder is a murder, and the law states...

(MAN threatens her with a 'revolver' in his jacket pocket)

3RD WOMAN. And that was how Kennedy left Parkland Hospital. It hardly needs saying that Mrs. Kennedy wanted to be alone for a little while. She opened the door of the sleeping cabin. There lay Johnson on her husband's bed...

MAN. Hi honey... (at a loss for words, thumps her on the back)... what do you say, Bird?

3RD WOMAN. I don't know what to say... what hurts me most of all, to tell you the truth, is that it should happen in Texas, my beloved Texas.

1ST WOMAN. Aren't we taking off soon?

MAN. I have to be sworn in first. There's Sarah, good old Sarah, Federal Judge in Texas. Come here.

(He stands so that 3RD WOMAN is on his left)

Come on, Jackie.

(1ST WOMAN stands on his right and 2ND WOMAN as Federal Judge in front of him)

3RD WOMAN. She has blood on her dress.

MAN. That's too bad. This is an important moment. (to an imaginary photographer) Just be careful you don't get too much on the picture.

3RD WOMAN. We're the presidential couple...

MAN. She's a Kennedy, can't you see?... Sarah...

no, for Christ's sake, we have no bible.

1ST WOMAN. There's one on my husband's bedside table.

2ND WOMAN. (takes a bible out of the chest) It's a Catholic one.

MAN. A bible is a bible. Come on, Sarah...

2ND WOMAN. I solemnly swear...

MAN. I solemnly swear...

2ND WOMAN. That I, and so on...

MAN. That I, and so on... so truly help me God. I thought of that last bit myself.

2ND WOMAN. Congratulations.

(Noise of engine starting on organ)

MAN. That's how to get on.

2ND WOMAN. I sit on the committee for a kindergarten for handicapped children. May I take the liberty of suggesting we rename it after your husband?

1ST WOMAN. That's very good of you.

(2ND WOMAN 'exits')

1ST WOMAN. The bible!

(Roar of a motor on the organ)

2ND WOMAN. At the foot of the landing steps Sarah was met by an authoritative man who asked her for the bible. She handed it to him mechanically thinking he must be a secret service man. He wasn't. In fact the Kennedy family bible disappeared without trace. It stayed in Dallas.

1ST WOMAN. They certainly needed it.

2ND WOMAN.
In Dallas where the hide's grown fast
Nearly every flag hung at half mast
Even the hard core did the same
From General Walker's house there came
The arm industry's cry, they said:
Hip hip hurrah, John Kennedy is dead.

1ST WOMAN.
Eleven schools laughed loud and sang
To think that such a stupid man
Had been shot at and died
And for the man who fired they cried
Each little hand above a head
Hip hip hurrah, John Kennedy is dead.

MAN.
It is the Lord God's work, you see
Now I'll trust in the Trinity
So cried a general standing there
And joyfully he ran home where
His wife put her arms round his head
Hug hug hurrah, John Kennedy is dead.

3RD WOMAN. Hello kids.

OTHERS. Hello Mom.

3RD WOMAN. I have the most marvellous news for

you. You know your big brother should have been going to Vietnam next month. Well, Daddy's arranged it all now. He's sending him to Paris for three years to study the history of the theatre.

MAN. Haven't you brought anything home for us, Mummy?

3RD WOMAN. Of course, sweetie pie. (she takes a box* , wrapped in pretty gift paper out of the chest) Just the thing for a clever little boy.

1ST WOMAN. Why is it always him that gets presents?

3RD WOMAN. It's for you girls as well. Come on, let's have some fun together.

(MAN unwraps the parcel. Inside the box there is a cardboard model)

MAN. Ooh! The little assassin. Thank you, Mummy.

3RD WOMAN. Let's see if you can get the hang of it. Open it here and then you can unfold it, that's the first thing to do. Then there are a whole lot of little bits here. Can you see what it is?

MAN. Yes, Mummy, it's Dealey Plaza. This goes

---

*Translator's Note

The cardboard model of Dealey Plaza, together with various other props used in the play and useful information can be found in 'The Assassination of President Kennedy' compiled and designed by Michael Rand, Howard Loxton and Len Deighton in the Jackdaw series, Jackdaw Publications.

on here, doesn't it? That's Main Street.

3RD WOMAN. That's right, with the criminal courts and the old courthouse.

MAN. That's the route the president took. It turns round here from Main Street right into Houston Street and then sharp left.

1ST WOMAN. Isn't it sweet? It even slopes properly.

2ND WOMAN. And here's the school book depository.

3RD WOMAN. Isn't it marvellous? That goes on here.

1ST WOMAN. Then the neon clock has to go on the top. Look how accurate it is; it says 12.30.

2ND WOMAN. Here's the car. Look, six little people. Isn't it terrific?

3RD WOMAN. We must put that here on Elm Street, after the bend.

2ND WOMAN. (pointing) What does the number one mean?

3RD WOMAN. That must be in the instructions.

1ST WOMAN. The position of Howard L. Brennan, the only eye witness who claimed to have seen Oswald firing from the window.

MAN. (in the 'witness box') When the president's car had passed me I heard an explosion. I thought it was someone throwing fireworks down from the book depository so I glanced up and there stood a man in the window on the sixth floor taking aim.

3RD WOMAN. (speaking as examining counsel) What kind of gun was it? Did it have a sight?

MAN. I didn't notice.

3RD WOMAN. What did the man look like?

MAN. He was in his early thirties, white, slender, nice-looking. He was wearing a light-coloured shirt, khaki colour. He was leaning out of the window and taking aim.

3RD WOMAN. Later that day you had to pick Oswald out from among six or seven other men. At first you said that you weren't sure. But a few days later you changed your mind.

MAN. Yes - I was afraid that it was a communist activity, so taking my family and myself into consideration - I, er - As soon as Oswald was killed there wasn't anything to be afraid of.

3RD WOMAN. Mr. Brennan, had you seen pictures of Oswald before you identified him?

MAN. Oh yes, I saw him on the television.

3RD WOMAN. I see. Thank you.

2ND WOMAN. Mummy, what does the number two mean, there on the road?

3RD WOMAN. Yes, what does it say about that?

1ST WOMAN. Move forward to two. This is the position of the president's car when the first shot was fired.

MAN. (clutches his neck) My God, I am hit.

2ND WOMAN. He didn't say anything.

3RD WOMAN. Yes he did. Kellerman was sitting on the front seat and heard it.

2ND WOMAN. A moment ago, you said that he didn't hear it.

3RD WOMAN. He heard it. It says so in the Warren Report. Move forward to three.

1ST WOMAN. The president is fatally wounded by the last shot.

2ND WOMAN. Then we go speeding along to the end and under the viaduct.

3RD WOMAN. (pointing at the map) Meanwhile Oswald hides the rifle and runs down into the lunch room on the second floor. Here he buys a cocacola out of the vending machine and soon after he leaves the book depository. He walks down Elm Street, catches a bus and travels back the same way he came. He changes to a taxi because of traffic hold-ups and six minutes later he's set down here and walks back to his room, where he changes his jacket. Fourteen minutes later Tippit stops his patrol car and is shot by Oswald who runs off in this direction and hides in a cinema without paying. Not long after the lights go up and the game is up. Oswald is overpowered and taken to the police station.

1ST WOMAN. How many shots were fired altogether?

3RD WOMAN. Most of the witnesses were of the same opinion, that they had heard three shots. Some, Mrs. Kennedy among them, said only two. Others heard four, five and six. You can understand how carefully the witnesses had to be examined.

1ST WOMAN. Presumably some bullets were found.

3RD WOMAN. Of course. In Parklands Hospital they found a whole bullet, and there were splinters of metal in Connally's wrist. And there were three empty cartridge cases by the window in the book depository.

MAN. Who says they were used? One could have been in the rifle when he came.

2ND WOMAN. Now she'll quote word for word.

3RD WOMAN. Nevertheless, the preponderance of the evidence led the Commission to conclude that there were three shots fired. One hit the president in the neck.

1ST WOMAN. (takes a picture from the chest) We have that here. (the picture, a drawing of the bullet's passage through the president's neck is shown as a slide) The actual X-ray photos have never been released, so you'll have to make do with a drawing. The bullet went in here, shattered the wind-pipe, and out the other side.

2ND WOMAN. How could he cry out that he'd been hit, then?

3RD WOMAN. He didn't. Mrs. Kennedy testifies that he didn't say anything. It says so in the

Report.

(New slide, Kennedy's jacket seen from behind)

1ST WOMAN. Here is his jacket. Notice how far down the hole is.

3RD WOMAN. Evidently the jacket slipped up when he was sitting with his hand raised.

(New slide, the shirt)

It seems that the hole is in the same position in the shirt, about six inches under the collar. Can a shirt slip that far up?

2ND WOMAN. Then there are the other two shots. One hit the president in the head.

(New slide, the injury to the brain)

It was that that killed him.

MAN. The other one hit Connally, then?

3RD WOMAN. No. One of the shots missed. Only two hit anything. The bullet that went through the president's neck carried on into Connally's back, bored through the right lung and came out just under the nipple, then went on through the wrist and finally ended up in the left thigh.

MAN. Could you explain that to me again?

(New slide, drawing of the path of the bullet)

1ST WOMAN. It's quite simple. Into the back of the president six inches under the collar, out of the neck, through the knot of the tie, into Connally's back, out through the breast, through the wrist into the thigh. This is what the wrist looked like afterwards.

(New slide, X-ray photo of the broken wrist)

MAN. It's easy to see why the bullet was splintered.

2ND WOMAN. Wasn't there a whole bullet found?

3RD WOMAN. Yes, on Connally's stretcher. The Commission concluded from that, that it had fallen out of the wound in his thigh.

1ST WOMAN. In order to make sure, they had to try and simulate the shot. So they shot a bullet of the same type through a dead goat, which was to represent Connally's chest. This is what it looked like afterwards.

(New slide, deformed bullet)

And they borrowed a cadaver and shot a bullet through the wrist.

(New slide, deformed bullet)

2ND WOMAN. But here it is, nice and clean - without any traces of blood or muscle.

(New slide, whole bullet)

MAN. Is there any more in the chest?

1ST WOMAN. Yes, Mr. Oswald, lots. (takes out a big sheet of paper) Now here's something for you, I think? An advertisement for Klein's sportshop?

Goodies from the army surplus stores. What about number three? A carbine with sight, 19.95, fast loading, fast firing, completely ready for use... tear here and send your order today.

3RD WOMAN. And that's exactly what he did. Not under his own name, of course. He used a pseudonym and had the weapon sent to a post box. So now all he has to do is get it into the book depository with him. - Mr. Frazier, when you drove to work and back you took Oswald with you in the car. That's what you did that Friday. He put an oblong package on the back seat, didn't he?

1ST WOMAN. (in the 'witness box') Yes. I said, what's in that?

MAN. Curtain rods.

1ST WOMAN. Oh. Where's your lunch-box? Did you forget it?

MAN. No, I thought I'd buy something.

3RD WOMAN. Notice that, please. He usually brought a lunch-box with him every day. What happened when you reached the parking lot?

1ST WOMAN. Well, we got out of the car.

3RD WOMAN. Did he wait for you?

1ST WOMAN. No, he went on ahead... with his package in his hand.

3RD WOMAN. And in your opinion, it was about 27 inches long?

1ST WOMAN. Yes, roughly that.

3RD WOMAN. On the fifth floor on the book depository a brown paperbag was found. It would fit a rifle, thirty-five inches long when it was stuck up. That's not so very different from twenty-seven. So the Commission concluded that the witness had misjudged the size.

MAN. But you remembered clearly enough how it was lying on the seat?

1ST WOMAN. Yes. It went from the arm rest to here. (shows what she means)

MAN. And that was measured by the police: twenty-seven inches. You remembered how I was carrying it too.

1ST WOMAN. (demonstrating) The top end was tucked in under his arm pit and he put his hand round the bottom end.

(2ND WOMAN takes the picture of the rifle out of the box of models, unfolds it and bends the top over)

2ND WOMAN. Here you are. Shall we take it apart and put it in the brown paperbag? That way we can make it that bit shorter.

(She helps MAN to hold it as described above. It won't fit)

1ST WOMAN. I'd like to hear what the arms experts have to say.

2ND WOMAN. (in the 'witness box') We positioned

three crack shots in a high tower, on the equivalent of the second floor. On the ground below we'd set up three cardboard figures as in Dallas. After we had adjusted the sights, the three marksmen were told to fire a series of three shots each.

1ST WOMAN. You adjusted the sights?

2ND WOMAN. Yes, the sight on Oswald's rifle was defective. We had to put three small iron wedges in.

1ST WOMAN. Is that so? What was the result, then?

2ND WOMAN. The best marksman managed to fire the three shots in 4.6 seconds. The others took more than five.

3RD WOMAN. How many times did these experts make a direct hit on the target?

2ND WOMAN. Not at all.

1ST WOMAN. I don't think we need to hear any more about the rifle, then.

MAN. Just one question. The officers who found the rifle wrote in their report that it was a Mauser. It remained a Mauser for two whole days. Then it suddenly became an Italian carbine. Who made them change their minds?

1ST WOMAN. And why?

3RD WOMAN. May I have the next slide?

(Slide, map of Dealey Plaza)

On this map of Dealey Plaza you can see a little Z. That's where Mr. Zapruder was standing with his cine camera, filming the whole assassination. Naturally the Commission made use of his film as important evidence.

(New slide, still number 193 from the film)

Here the president's car has turned into Elm Street, followed by the secret service car. You must excuse the slight lack of clarity.

2ND WOMAN. As a matter of fact it's a copy. Life came along first and bought the original.

(New slide from the film)

Now the car's turning round by the road sign.

(New slide from film)

Here the president is stooping forward again. Notice how he's clutching at his neck - on the next picture one can see...

(Quick, flickering series of slides)

... quite clearly, that governor Connally has been hit too. Thank you. When a film is running at eighteen frames a second we can establish an exact time sequence. The president and Connally are hit on frame 210 and the next shot hits home on picture number 313. That's easily five seconds between the first and the second shot, much more than Oswald needs.

MAN. Three years after the murder Life Magazine came to visit Connally. Mr. Connally, you were not in complete agreement with the Commission?

2ND WOMAN. No, but it's pretty difficult to see while the film is running.

MAN. Life has made an enlargement of every single frame. (he passes her a pile of pictures) Here you are just past the sign post. You're sitting with your head turned to the right. The president's been hit.

2ND WOMAN. I turned round when I heard the shot, and I managed to turn right round before I was hit. I remember it was like a blow of the fist on my back. Here - it's here I was hit. Perhaps a frame before.

MAN. And are you sure about that?

2ND WOMAN. Yes.

MAN. That's twenty-four frames after the first shot, the equivalent of 1.3 seconds. So Connally was hit 1.3 seconds after the president.

3RD WOMAN. No, because Oswald's rifle couldn't shoot that fast. You were hit by the same shot.

MAN. Are you suggesting that the bullet took 1.3 seconds to pass through Kennedy? Don't you think it's more likely that there were two assassins shooting at almost the same time?

3RD WOMAN. Or a whole gang?

1ST WOMAN. Why not? You forgot to say what happened while Oswald was changing his jacket in his room. A patrol car drove up and stopped outside. It stood there for a little while and hooted a couple of times then drove off again.

2ND WOMAN. And while we're talking about hooting, who was it that gave a signal on his horn just before Oswald was shot by Ruby?

3RD WOMAN. The whole book depository was obviously occupied by assassins.

MAN. Why only the book depository? Put yourself here where Kennedy was shot. On this spot settler Bryan knocked a post into the ground in 1841 and round it Dallas grew up. So what do we have within rifle range? A kindergarten, a hidden gambling den, a convent, a whorehouse, a building site, Ruby's nightclub - that's places enough.

1ST WOMAN. (with the model) The slope down Elm Street, for example. At the top by the railings we have a little figure four: 'here eight witnesses noticed a cloud of smoke'.

2ND WOMAN. And there were foot-prints in the mud.

MAN. There were traces of both lead and copper in the wrist. In the brain wound there was only lead... as if it had come from a dum-dum bullet.

1ST WOMAN. You had to find the truth and you had to put an end to rumours - you were so busy dealing with the latter that you failed to achieve the former.

2ND WOMAN.
Johnson said to Warren

I have need of you.

MAN.
Warren said Good mornin'
I don't care if you do.

2ND WOMAN.
Johnson thumped the table
You'll do as I say.

MAN.
Warren found he was able
Johnson's part to play.

2ND WOMAN.
To recreate the nation's
Former peace of mind.

MAN.
That was the Commission's
First answer to find.

2ND WOMAN.
It'll make me look keen
Help in my career.

MAN.
That way keep your slate clean
From the blame you fear.

2ND WOMAN.
You understand the project
Now go and do the work.

MAN.
I see no cause to object
As long as I don't shirk
The task of Madame Justice

Whose honour I uphold.

2ND WOMAN.
Don't worry, since the fact is
That she wears a blindfold.

3RD WOMAN. If Oswald wasn't the murderer, who was, then?

MAN. That's exactly what the Commission should have found out.

1ST WOMAN. We don't know. But perhaps a more likely question is, who could have been the murderer. Whom can we find motives for? Shall we try?

MAN. (naively pleased) You can say what you like about Kennedy, I now maintain he was an idealist. Do you realize he never received any salary in his public offices? Neither as a senator or as president? He made the whole lot over to charity.

3RD WOMAN. Yes, that was a beautiful gesture.

MAN. It certainly was.

3RD WOMAN. That's just what I'm saying.

MAN. No, you're not. It _was_ a beautiful gesture.

1ST WOMAN. What about the grocer's bill?

MAN. What?

1ST WOMAN. He must have earned some money. A summer house at Cape Cod, a private jet, a villa on the Riviera, expensive works of art, a lot of travelling - where did the money come from?

3RD WOMAN. He played the stock market.

MAN. Oh, no, not Kennedy.

2ND WOMAN. Unearned income, my friend. The whole thing started when the potato crop failed in Ireland in 1850. Grandpa packed up and went to the States. Good old Honey Fitz laid the foundations and daddy Joe knew enough to carry on building.

(She fishes a big cigar and the Financial Times out of the chest)

Yellow Cab doesn't look too happy.

1ST WOMAN. Bad is it?

2ND WOMAN. On its last legs. (moves the cigar thoughtfully over to the other corner of her mouth) It was a good firm once, you know.

1ST WOMAN. What's the matter with it?

2ND WOMAN. No one's dealing in it. The price is right down to 52. It's got the plague all right.

1ST WOMAN. That's sad.

(2ND WOMAN laughs noisily)

1ST WOMAN. I said that's sad.

2ND WOMAN. Why?

1ST WOMAN. I mean, if it goes bankrupt now... ?

2ND WOMAN. You've a lot to learn. (cigar over to the other corner of her mouth) Do you want to make some money?

1ST WOMAN. Of course. How?

2ND WOMAN. Gamble.

1ST WOMAN. Poker?

2ND WOMAN. Yellow Cab.

1ST WOMAN. Yellow Cab?

2ND WOMAN. Mm. It won't go bankrupt. Well, not immediately anyway.

1ST WOMAN. O.K., then, let's get going.

(2ND WOMAN shakes her head)

1ST WOMAN. (after a pause) What are we waiting for?

2ND WOMAN. A drop.

(3RD WOMAN sits behind the chest, takes a pile of printed paper out of it, as well as the Financial Times and a ticker. The MAN is given the newspaper)

We're off, then. You go to the stock market and buy a share.

1ST WOMAN. (goes over to the chest) Where is Yellow Cab standing?

3RD WOMAN. Pretty low, it's down to 48.

1ST WOMAN. Pretty low. I'll have one.

3RD WOMAN. Nominal value 1000 dollars, buyable for 480.

1ST WOMAN. Thank you. (back to 2ND WOMAN) That was my trick, now it's you to play.

(2ND WOMAN shakes her head)

MAN. (goes over to chest) I fancy buying a share, just a little one. Isn't there something called Yellow Cab?

3RD WOMAN. I'd really advise you against that, sir. It's down to 48. There's bankruptcy on the horizon. Boeing's better.

MAN. I'll think it over.

2ND WOMAN. No it's my turn. (goes over to chest) Yellow Cab.

3RD WOMAN. You shouldn't, you know.

2ND WOMAN. (whispers) I have faith in Yellow Cab.

3RD WOMAN. Oh yes? One?

2ND WOMAN. One thousand.

3RD WOMAN. Yeees. The nominal value is 1000. You get it for 480.

2ND WOMAN. I want to buy one thousand.

3RD WOMAN. One thousand shares?

2ND WOMAN. Yes.

3RD WOMAN. (confidentially) Is something happening to Yellow Cab?

2ND WOMAN. I'm not saying anything. Will you take a cheque?

3RD WOMAN. Naturally Mr. Kennedy. 480,000.

(2ND WOMAN takes 1000 shares, hides 999 of them and shows one to 1ST WOMAN)

2ND WOMAN. Now I've bought one too.

MAN. (read'ng) Amalgamated aggravator, devaluating devastator, co-operating copulator, Yellow Cab.

3RD WOMAN. Large market in Yellow Cab.

(The machine ticks, tape runs out)

MAN. I think I'll have one just the same.

3RD WOMAN. Here you are. That's 490.

MAN. 90?

3RD WOMAN. The price has risen. But that's a good sign, sir, decidedly.

MAN. I'll spoil myself and buy two, then.

3RD WOMAN. Here you are.

2ND WOMAN. (to 1ST WOMAN) You to play. I'd like to buy that one from you, so I'll pay with this one. All right?

(They exchange shares. The machine ticks. 3RD WOMAN stares at it, kisses the tape)

1ST WOMAN. Ah ha!

3RD WOMAN. Dealing in Yellow Cab again.

MAN. Is that a good sign? Then I'll have two more. Twice 490 is...

3RD WOMAN. Twice 500, the price is rising. But that's marvellous.

MAN. Then I'd better have four.

(He takes four. 1ST and 2ND WOMAN exchange their shares again, several times. The machine ticks, the tape crawls out and 3RD WOMAN caresses it lasciviously)

MAN. Amalgamated aggravator, vietnamaking decimator, Yellow Cab. Large sales, what's their value now?

3RD WOMAN. 52.

MAN. I'll take six.

(He takes six. 1ST and 2ND WOMAN exchange shares to and fro. The machine ticks like mad and 3RD WOMAN slides the tape amorously between her breasts)

MAN. (reading) Amalgagagagagaga - Yellow Cab -

trade today reached the most lively level so far.

3RD WOMAN. It's up to 60.

MAN. I'd better have ten.

3RD WOMAN. Perhaps they'll go up again tomorrow.

(The two WOMEN exchange shares faster and faster, the machine ticks like a lunatic)

MAN. O hell, I'll take 100. That's 60,000 dollars, isn't it?

3RD WOMAN. 70. The price is going up.

(The MAN considers. The two WOMEN exchange shares even faster, the machine ticks frantically. 3RD WOMAN puts the tape between her thighs and rubs it)

3RD WOMAN. The tendency is rising strongly.

2ND WOMAN. They're saying in well-informed financial circles...

1ST WOMAN. It's hinted from reliable sources...

3RD WOMAN. You can make a fortune sir, if you're quick about it.

MAN. O.K. I'll sink everything I have into it. That's all my savings. (he takes 1000 shares)

3RD WOMAN. 85,000, thank you.

2ND WOMAN. The price is up to 85, then. O.K., we're selling. (she lays the 1000 shares on the chest)

3RD WOMAN. That's 850,000 for you.

1ST WOMAN. What's that? you didn't say anything about that.

2ND WOMAN. Well, now you know.

1ST WOMAN. Anyway there should be 850 for me.

3RD WOMAN. Unfortunately only 600. The Price has just fallen.

(1ST WOMAN is furious with 2ND WOMAN)

2ND WOMAN. What are you sulking for? You've made 120 dollars in a week. That's five pounds a day without taking your hands out of your pockets.

MAN. (referring to the ticker) Won't it go any more?

3RD WOMAN. It's coming to pieces, sir, I'm very sorry.

(MAN throws his shares out over the audience. Then takes a revolver from the chest)

1ST WOMAN. Who might think of murdering Kennedy?

(MAN takes a sign out of the chest and hangs it up. It reads 'The Exploited?')

1ST WOMAN. And who else?

MAN. Oh, I don't know...I should think there are

masses of them. Let's sing our song. (he hands Latin American rhythm instruments round to the others)

CHORUS.

Down in Guatemala
Fideliy, Fidelay, Fidel Castro
Down in Guatemala was a camp all hidden away
Where soldiers lived and waited in their hope for
(victory day
Kennedy lent them weapons, bullets by the ton
They practised under cover and learned to use a
(gun
Training and money were given by a firm
(called C.I.A.
Finally came their important and anxiously
(waited day
The White House had sent orders that they should
(show their hand
Cubans in exile all thought that freedom would come
(to their land
We're coming right now, old pal Castro, to have a
(good tug at your beard
With our Yankee machines we are ready to fight
(everything we once feared
Kennedy slept in his mansion while his soldiers wer
(creeping to land
Castro, on his side more watchful, chased them
(back across the sand
The Bay of Pigs was a fiasco, and Kennedy's plans
(come to nought
But at least the free world had done something,
(since it had been for freedom they fought.

1ST WOMAN. Who might think of murdering Kennedy?

(She hangs up a sign reading 'The Cubans?')

MAN. Or these, because he didn't help them enough.

(He hangs up a sign reading 'Cuban Exiles?'. 3RD WOMAN takes a book from the chest)

3RD WOMAN. In 1962 the Russians established rocket bases in Cuba. We quote from Kennedy's speech of the time: 'Several of them include medium range ballistic missiles capable of carrying a nuclear warhead for a distance of more than one thousand nautical miles. Each of these missiles, in short, is capable of striking Washington D.C., The Panama Canal, Cape Canaveral, Mexico City or any other city in the Southeastern part of the United States.

(Slide, map of America with rocket striking distances marked)

MAN. As you may perhaps remember, President Kennedy forced Khruschev to dismantle these threatening bases.

2ND WOMAN. Perhaps we should see the whole map?

(New slide: both continents with the striking range of the U.S. rockets in Turkey marked)

Those bases weren't removed.

1ST WOMAN. Who might think of murdering Kennedy?

(She takes a sign out of the chest and hangs it up. It reads 'The Russians?')

2ND WOMAN. Senator Fulbright, you are a spokesman on foreign policy and known as an unbiased and fair-minded politician. What is your opinion about the stream of refugees going from East to West Germany, who now in 1961 number thousands every day?

MAN. I don't understand why the East Germans don't close their frontiers.

2ND WOMAN. Isn't that a bold statement from a politician?

MAN. It's the truth.

1ST WOMAN. Naturally. No country can afford to lose so much labour and so much brain power.

3RD WOMAN. And no one can reproach these people for choosing the West.

1ST WOMAN. Of course not. Which one of us can resist a temptation like that. Das Wirtschaftswunder - von U.S.A. bezahlt. (The Economic Miracle - subsidized by the U.S.A.)

2ND WOMAN. So you think it would be understandable if the East Germans closed their border?

MAN. Yes.

2ND WOMAN. Supposing they do this - what kind of stand would we take, then?

MAN. None at all. The East Germans are well within their rights.

1ST WOMAN. And so they built the wall.

3RD WOMAN. Tragic.

1ST WOMAN. Indeed yes... but perhaps understandable all the same, if you're prepared to admit it.

3RD WOMAN. Kennedy saw the wall himself, two years later.

MAN. (delivering a speech) There are many people in the world who really don't understand, or say they don't, what is the great issue between the free world and the Communist world. Let them come to Berlin. There are some who say that Communism is the wave of the future. Let them come to Berlin. And there are some who say in Europe and elsewhere that we can work with the Communists. Let them come to Berlin... All free men, wherever they may live, are citizens of Berlin, and therefore as a free man I take pride in the words: Ich bin ein Berliner.

(Noisy cheering and applause)

1ST WOMAN. Mightn't they have reason to murder Kennedy? (she hangs up a sign reading 'Communists?')

2ND WOMAN. (with a book) Here is another quotation: 'But American military might should not and need not stand alone against the ambitions of international Communism... that is why our military and economic assistance plays such a key role in enabling those who live on the periphery of the Communist world to maintain their independence of choice. Our assistance to these nations can be painful, risky and costly as is true in South East Asia today. But we dare not weary of the task. Our assistance makes possible the stationing of 4½ million Allied troops along the

Communist frontier...

MAN. At one tenth the cost of maintaining a comparable number of American soldiers.

(Film with pictures of Vietnam; contrast between maimed children and smiling officers and politicians. At the end a father with his dead son in his arms)

Ich bin ein Vietnameser.

(Film ends. Fade in over Vietnam film of Kennedy with his beautifully dressed son in his arms)

1ST WOMAN. Who might think of killing Kennedy?

(3RD WOMAN takes sign from her)

3RD WOMAN.
Why go meddling with a myth even though it looks (too clean
Why all these aggressive words, why start out to (be so mean
Why all these sarcastic sneers, this nasty dirty (smell
Why the man who only had a short chance to do (well
Why not round the other way
Ask the ones who had to stay
Since they made sure the myth was passed intact (to us today
Why did you all fail to pay
Homage to the blood that may
Have proved a source to be tapped by those who (thought the same way?
Why not just as quietly see by looking in his eyes

That power couldn't tempt a man like him into
(disdain and lies
Why not try less for just this once to cut him
(down to size
But look again at what he said and realize what
(was wise
He was not a petty man
Look how far his influence ran
Remember that the world still needs someone to
(build a span
Especially the American
Who thinks that many problems can
Be solved without much trouble by killing his
(fellow man.

(She takes the book)

Another quotation: The denial of constitutional rights to some of our fellow Americans on account of race... subjects us to the charge of world opinion that our democracy is not equal to the high promise of our heritage.

(They all put photo-masks on, the MAN as a negro, the others white)

3RD WOMAN. We take an incident reported in Life magazine.

MAN. When I asked for coffee, the good lady said she couldn't serve me.

3RD WOMAN. We'll serve you if you can just keep quiet - but it'll be out of the goodness of our hearts.

MAN. I cannot tell you how I felt.

2ND WOMAN. I love my country but when those guys in the government start telling me what I can and can't do in my own place then that's Communism.

1ST WOMAN. Give them an inch and they'll take a mile. I've seen them up North. They walk along the pavement four by four and shove the whites out into the gutter.

2ND WOMAN. I'm going to sell out and move to Russia. There's more freedom over there.

MAN. I was astounded and angry. But President Kennedy made me an apology.

3RD WOMAN. He looked like an ordinary dirty nigger. How was I to know that he was an ambassador from Africa.

(They put the masks down. 3RD WOMAN hangs up a sign reading 'Kukluxklan?')

1ST WOMAN. Sarah, what happened about your plans to call the kindergarten after my husband?

2ND WOMAN. The motion was defeated, Mrs. Kennedy. 72 votes to 52.

(1ST WOMAN takes some pieces of paper from MAN's inside pocket)

1ST WOMAN. This is the speech you should have made before the business men of Dallas: 'But today other voices are heard in the land - voices preaching doctrines wholly unrelated to reality... doctrines which apparently assume that words will suffice without weapons, that vituperation is as good as victory and that peace is a sign of weakness'. I think I know whom you were talking about.

(During the following song, which can be sung by one or more of the actors, a primitive cartoon film is shown to fit the words)

With a little cunning
You can make your money
Multiply right now
Listen and we'll tell you how
And it won't cost you money

Almost without thinking
Since it's easy as winking
I muster what I've saved
Then I know the way is paved
No fear of my cash shrinking

Seven per cent's a fraction
Of what a little action
Can easily bring your way
Use what brains you have today
Abandon all inaction

The answer's in the soil
A certain source of oil
And down with my drill
My machines are never still
I keep them on the boil.

When the oil's flowing
The pump is to-and-fro-ing
I buy another rig
All I have to do is dig
The wind of wealth is blowing

If you can see my logic

And follow the mechanics
Of money-making schemes
You'll know that I've no time for dreams
But must alter my tactics

No room for complaining
There're other ways of gaining
I'll buy some factory shares
It's a trick that one who cares
Knows is worth maintaining

For a thousand they're going
My shares, because they're Boeing
And war has been declared
So though a partial slump is feared
My cup is overflowing

The fatherland is calling
The sound of shells appalling
My duty heavy lies
My salty tears blind my eyes
When I hear my bombs falling

But when we learn that peace is
Come the bombing ceases
Profit from arms must stop
All attempts to reap the crop
Of war have gone to pieces

There's no need to worry
Though I have to hurry
And start another war
A cheap one smaller than before
And trade is all a flurry.

And so the situation
Is stable, with rotation
We have wars every day

The Pentagon and C. I. A.
Should share the acclamation.

(Towards the end of the film, three signs are hung up, reading 'C. I. A. ?', 'Pentagon?' and 'The Arms Industry?'. 3RD WOMAN takes a letter out of the chest)

3RD WOMAN. Secret Service, March 1st, 1964. The chief of the Criminal Section in Dallas reveals that Lee Harvey Oswald was on the pay roll of the F. B. I. for a salary of 200 dollars a month. - That's the latest.

(They lift up the chest and turn it over so that it can be seen to be empty)

2ND WOMAN. (sings)
Nineteen sixty-eight
Dallas free of hate
The murder's been forgotten, the years carry (their own weight

For Dallas a fresh start
Elm Street's almost smart
But underneath the clean facade there beats a (stony heart.

MAN. You see, in New Orleans there's a district attorney called Jim Garrison. He's six foot six inches tall - though that has nothing to do with the story.

(Sings)

Big Jim Garrison, so they say,
Set his mind to working.
Jim's a good lawyer any day

But suspicions were lurking
The lines on which his thinking ran
Concerned the pointless killing
The President was a great man
His memory should be living.

CHORUS.

Allelujah - America shakes its head
Allelujah - America's weeping.

MAN.

Jim begins all on his own
Using his bare hands
Slowly till his work's so grown
That he can find loose ends.
The thread twists taut without a knot
Until the yarn is tightening
Dimly Jim perceives the plot
Which may well be enlightening.

CHORUS.

Allelujah - America shakes its head
Allelujah - America's smiling.

MAN.

Suddenly a witness died,
The court with questions filled
Did he kill himself?, they cried
Or was he maybe killed?
In his left hand he held the gun
Though alive he used his right
The trial should, said Jim for one
Be brought into daylight.

CHORUS.

Allelujah - America shakes its head
Allelujah - America's yawning.

MAN.

Jim says that yet another guy
Was crashed from air to land
While one more had no need to fly
But met a well-aimed hand
Fourteen deaths in various places
All very hard to swallow
Nicely veil the slender traces
Jim is trying to follow.

CHORUS.

Allelujah - Jim Garrison shakes his head
Allelujah - Jim Garrison's smiling.

MAN.

As far as I'm concerned churchyards
Can fill and overflow
I have put people behind bars
Because of what I know.

(Piercing ring as from a telephone. Music stops)

2ND WOMAN. Hello?

VOICE. Is that Mrs. Garrison?

2ND WOMAN. Yes.

VOICE. You have small children, don't you? We'll be laying hands on them on the way home from school. Regards to the creole swine. (click)

MAN. That's me.

2ND WOMAN. Jim, are you considering the children?

MAN. (sings)

That is just what's in my mind

I'd be a disgrace
If one day I chanced to find
Untruth in my own face.

CHORUS.
Allelujah - America shakes its head
Allelujah - America's laughing.

(A letter falls onto the stage)

2ND WOMAN. It's for you.

1ST WOMAN. (reads) Dear Mrs. Kennedy, we are a cross section of business people in Dallas who are worried by our decreasing trade with other states. We would be very glad if you would sign your name on the enclosed certificate of Dallas' hospitality.